CW00864883

Call of the Desert

The Sahara

All photographs in this book are by Philippe Bourseiller, with the exception of Philippe Bourseiller's portrait on page 10.

Translation for the English language edition: Chris Miller
Typesetting for the English language edition: Christophe Tardieux

ISBN 0-8109-5978-X

Published in 2005 by Harry N. Abrams, Incorporated, New York

Printed and bound in Belgium.
10 9 8 7 6 5 4 3 2 1

Abrams is a subsidiary of

Call of the Desert
The Sahara

Photographs by
Philippe Bourseiller

Text by
Catherine Guigon

Drawings by
Virginie Van den Bogaert

HARRY N. ABRAMS, INC. PUBLISHERS

CONTENTS

The Sahara beckons...

The Sahara Desert is very, very big. If you really want to know what it's like, it's not enough to pop over to Africa for a week or two. It took the photographer Philippe Plisson twenty-five trips over the course of four years to collect the images that you see in this book. That meant 70,000 kilometres of dirt tracks and more than his share of sandstorms.

Now, Philippe Plisson is something of an adventurer. He likes to be near volcanoes or ice-floes, and he was bound to come up against the Sahara desert sooner or later. The first time he did, he nearly got lost and soon realised he needed to improve his navigational skills! But the desert captured his imagination. This book is the result of a project he began in 2001. He decided to criss-cross the Sahara in every direction, spending weeks at a time in the desert so that he could really take in the atmosphere of the many places he visited. That meant scouring the ten different countries over which the desert extends, waiting for the right light in order to capture perfect images of these spectacular landscapes.

If you wanted to do the same, you'd have to be well prepared. You would need a four-by-four to travel in, and you would certainly have to take a local guide. You would have to carry your own food and stock up on water in a big way. You don't find many petrol pumps in the desert, so you would have to carry two-hundred-litre petrol cans. The food would have to be dry food because it keeps better: rice and pasta. You would be able to buy fresh vegetables from time to time in oases.

Then you would have to do some serious planning. It would be best to go to the Sahara during the "winter", which lasts from October to March. The heat is less intense then, there are fewer sandstorms, and the colour of the sky is a more radiant blue. You would have to be prepared for extremes of temperature, all the same. In the Sudan, for example, the temperature can still go as high as forty-five degrees centigrade, even in winter. But the night is very cold in the desert, especially in the mountains. In the Hoggar region (in Algeria), it can fall below minus eighty-eight degrees centigrade. So you'll need the right clothes: a windproof jacket, a fleece, cool cotton trousers, and—a real "must"—sunglasses. You also need a warm sleeping bag. All this you must carry in a rucksack. Some things must be carefully sealed against the sand. You know what sand is like, it gets everywhere, and it's not very good for cameras!

You might travel for three days just to reach your destination. Then, if you're lucky, your guide will set up camp for you and you can wander off—not too far!—and scout the area for things to photograph. But be careful, night falls suddenly. Dawn is a great time for taking photographs.

You would have to get used to your own company. You and your guide are going to spend a long time without meeting anyone else. But eventually you will meet up with some nomads. You are unlikely to know their language but that may not matter. Communication is possible. These people may not be as rich as you are, but their hospitality is wonderful. They live here. This is their home. Learn from them, if you can.

All right. Are you ready? Let's go!

The Sahara Desert

The Climate of the Sahara:
The Sahara has a desert climate. This means very high air temperatures (40°centigrade plus) and little or no water. The Sahara has 3,400 hours of sunlight per year compared to around 1,750 for the United Kingdom. Only 250 millimetres of water fall per year. The desert is swept by hot winds such as the Harmattan and the Sirocco.

The Landscape of the Sahara:
Many people think that the Sahara is all sand. In fact, stretches of shifting sand (*ergs*) occupy only a quarter of the Sahara's ten million square kilometres. Much of the desert consists of *regs*, vast areas covered in small stones. The Sahara also has mountainous areas, called *massifs*, forming a "spine" that runs roughly east-west. These include the Ahaggar (highest point: Mount Tahat, 2,908 metres above sea-level), the Aïr (Mount Bagzane, 2,202 metres), the Tibesti (Emi Koussi, 3,415 metres) and the Ennedi (Mount Basso, 1,450 metres).

The Peoples of the Sahara:
Despite the difficult climate, many peoples live in the Sahara. They include Maures (in Mauritania), Tuaregs (Algeria, Niger and Mali) and Toubous (Chad). These nomadic peoples cover great distances with their camels searching for water or transporting goods in caravans. In the south, in the semi-desert zone of the Sahel, live the Peul Bororos. They breed cattle and lead their herds in search of pasture during the rainy season.

The Animal Life of the Sahara:
All kinds of creatures have acclimatised to the Sahara, they have learnt to live there. Snakes and scorpions are commonest, because they are best adapted to the heat. There are also mammals such as the gazelle, the addax antelope and the fennec, a little desert fox. In the cooler air of the Tibesti mountains, monkeys are found. Larks and white-rumped black wheatears nest in oases.

The Plant Life of the Sahara:
Plants are rare in the desert, which is too dry for them to flourish. But their seeds, hidden in the soil, germinate at the first drop of rain. As many as 600 species of flowering plant have been found in Tibesti (Chad) compared to just seven in the Tanezrouft region of Mauritania. A few trees grow in the Sahara, notably tamarisk and acacia.

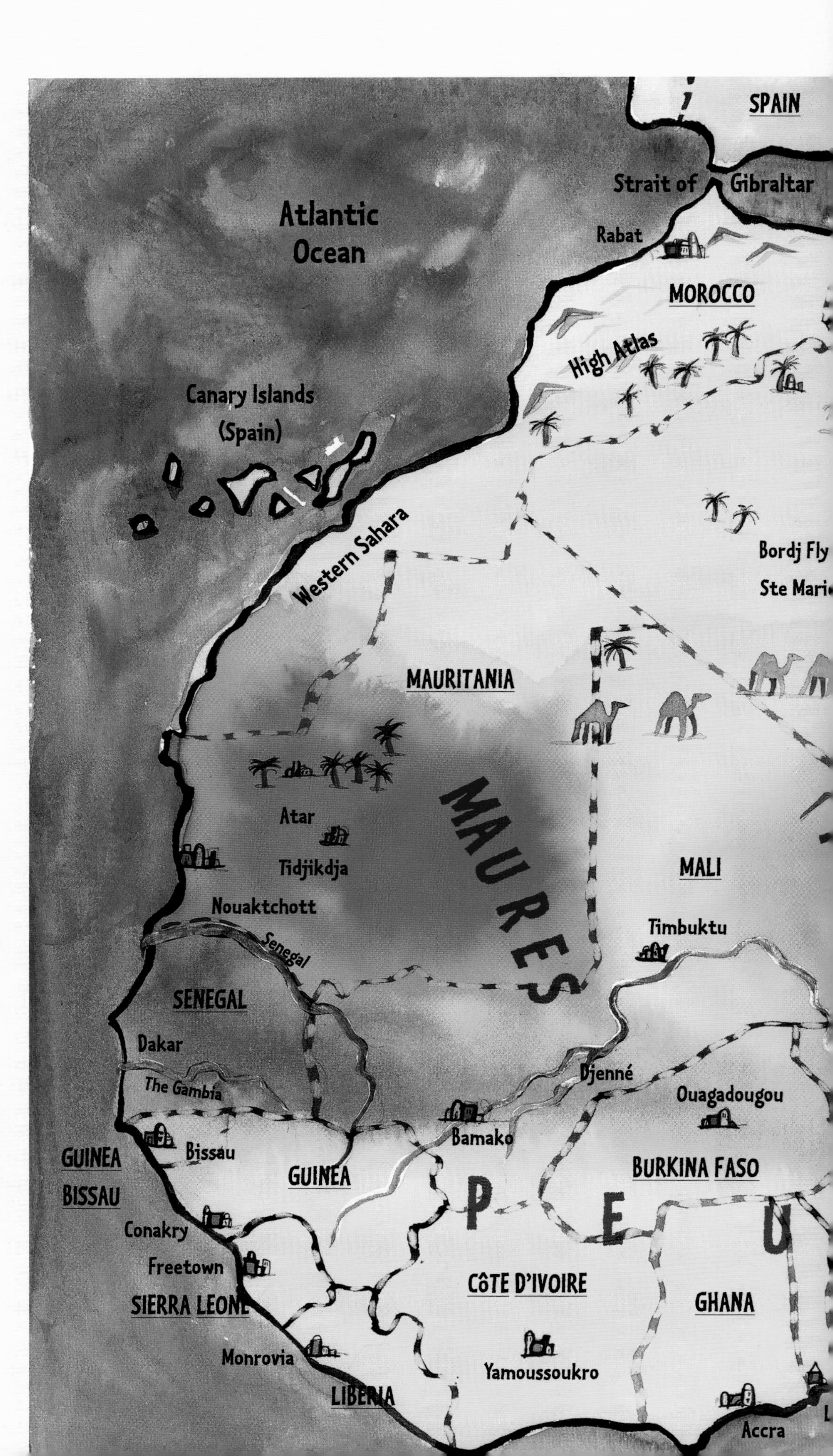

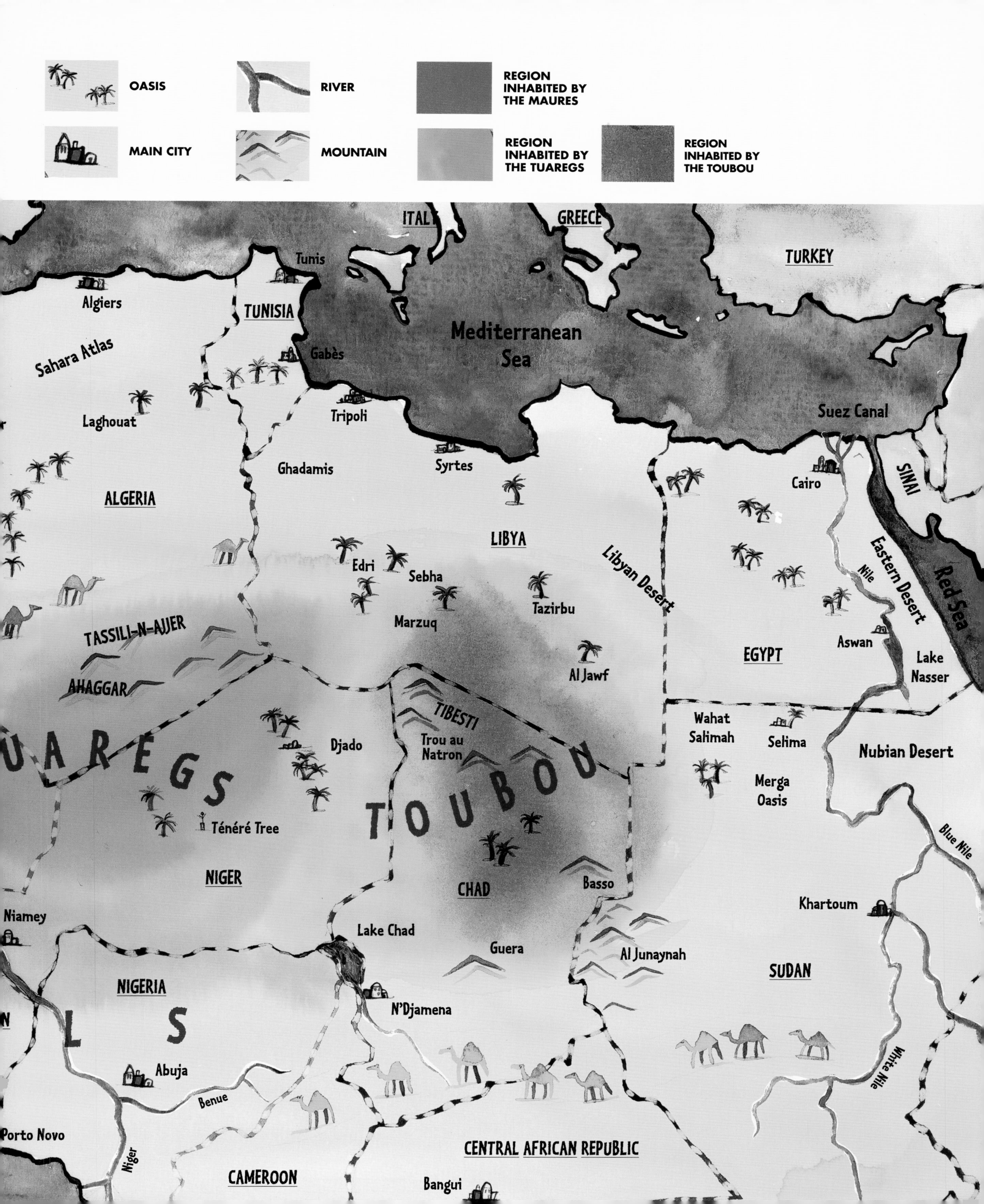
OASIS
RIVER
REGION INHABITED BY THE MAURES
MAIN CITY
MOUNTAIN
REGION INHABITED BY THE TUAREGS
REGION INHABITED BY THE TOUBOU
ITALY
GREECE
TURKEY
Tunis
Algiers
TUNISIA
Mediterranean Sea
Sahara Atlas
Gabès
Laghouat
Tripoli
Suez Canal
Ghadamis
Syrtes
Cairo
SINAI
ALGERIA
LIBYA
Libyan Desert
Eastern Desert
Red Sea
Nile
Edri
Sebha
Tazirbu
Marzuq
TASSILI-N-AJJER
Aswan
EGYPT
Lake Nasser
Al Jawf
AHAGGAR
TIBESTI
Wahat Salimah
Selima
Nubian Desert
UAREGS
Djado
Trou au Natron
TOUBOU
Merga Oasis
Ténéré Tree
Blue Nile
NIGER
CHAD
Basso
Khartoum
Niamey
Lake Chad
Guera
Al Junaynah
NIGERIA
SUDAN
N'Djamena
N L S
Abuja
White Nile
Benue
Porto Novo
Niger
CENTRAL AFRICAN REPUBLIC
CAMEROON
Bangui

Faces of the Sahara

Towering rocks and sand dunes stretch away as far as the eye can see. This is a barren world, sun-baked and hostile to life—unless, of course, there is water, as here in the Ennedi region, where the palm trees mark an oasis.

The Sahara is the biggest desert in the world. At ten million square kilometres, it is well over forty times the size of Great Britain! Lying in the tropics, it forms a long arid strip that stretches across the entire continent of Africa, from the Atlantic in the west to the Red Sea in the east, through ten countries: Mauritania, Morocco, Algeria, Mali, Niger, Libya, Tunisia, Chad, Sudan and Egypt.

Like all deserts, the Sahara has almost no water. In some places, rain simply never falls. The dryness and fierce sunlight—the temperature can reach seventy degrees centigrade—eliminate most forms of life. These spectacular landscapes are made of nothing but stone and sand. Some regions of the Sahara are less dry, such as the banks of the Nile in Egypt and the parts of Niger watered by the river that gave the country its name.

Yet some people do live in the Sahara. Many of them are nomads like the Tuaregs and Toubou, travelling on camels from well to well or oasis to oasis in search of grazing for their animals. Others, like the Peul Bororo, will stay in one place for a time before moving on. Following the rains in their quest for fresh pastures, these peoples have tamed the desert.

Ergs—vast areas covered by sand dunes—constitute only a small part of the Sahara.

Tuareg Festival

For the festival of Tafsit, held at Tamanrasset in Algeria, Tuaregs dressed in their most colourful costumes converge from every direction: from Algeria, Mali, Niger and Chad. Some 400,000 Tuaregs still live as nomads.

Tuareg men never appear in public with their face uncovered. This prohibition only affects men, for whom wearing a sort of veil is a sign of courtesy and respect, particularly toward tribal Elders. The veil is a huge length of cloth—it can be as much as five metres long—called the *taguelmoust*. It requires considerable skill to drape it around the head so that it stays on. Black, white or burgundy are the everyday colours, but for festivals an indigo *taguelmoust* is worn. Indigo is a natural dark-blue dye with violet overtones; the plant from which it is made is increasingly rare. The dye is expensive but easily comes off on one's hands—which is why these noble desert warriors were once known as "the blue men".

By contrast, Tuareg women are never required to veil their faces. This is very unusual among Islamic peoples and is a case where Tuareg traditions have taken precedence over Islamic customs. Islam permits men to have several wives, but Tuareg custom allows men to have only one. Married women express themselves freely in the family and in public, and this too is exceptional.

Traditional silver Tuareg jewelry.

Adapting to the Climate

How small and vulnerable this crow seems as he perches on top of a dune. Surely he will die of thirst? No. Birds, reptiles, insects and a few mammals have adapted to the furnace-like conditions of the Sahara. Gazelles, for example, can survive on very little water.

Crows are strange birds. They seem at home anywhere in the world, as happy in deserts as in milder regions. They are not afraid of the heat and seem able to find an insect or sprig of vegetation even in an area of shifting dunes (called an *erg*) like the Libyan Murzuq seen here. Crows are not the only birds found in the Sahara. Predators like vultures and eagle-owls fly over the sands, while smaller birds—like the white-rumped black wheatear—live in oases. Tuaregs call the wheatear *moula-moula*. They are very fond of it since the sight of it means that they are close to water.

Insects and reptiles protect themselves from the sun by going underground. Scorpions seek the shelter of stones and snakes burrow into the sand. In this way they can survive temperatures of fifty degrees centigrade or more. They hunt smaller creatures, snakes, for example, kill and eat desert rodents.

Some mammals are equally well equipped to survive the desert life. The fennec is a nocturnal fox whose large ears allow it to track the small animals it feeds on by listening for the slightest sounds they make as they scuttle across the sands. During the day, the fennec sleeps underground in its deep burrow. The herds of graceful gazelles count on their speed to take them out of danger quickly.

Gazelles were once numerous. Now, they are an endangered species.

Dead of Thirst

Intense heat killed this young camel. He died of dehydration, no longer having enough water in his body to remain on his feet. His bones now bleach in the sun.

Some regions of the Sahara are merciless. One such region is the east of Mauritania, where this animal died. The Madjabat-el-Koubra desert stretches away some 1,700 kilometres into the distance and the nearest water is some 900 kilometres away.

In 1954, the famous French explorer and naturalist Théodore Monod was the first European to cross this desert. He was accompanied by two local guides. They took with them five camels and all their food and water. Monod steered by the compass and drank only half a litre of water a day in order not to exhaust his supply. His expedition lasted nearly two months.

Even today there are few more perilous places than Madjabat-el-Koubra. The dangers have been reduced by satellite navigation and mobile phones, but the unexpected may still strike. A Saharan proverb tells us that "Fortune is master of the desert—and desert fortune is always bad". So take care!

In the desert, water is a precious commodity. Here nomads mingle around a well.

An Open-Air School

A blackboard, a bit of chalk, a teacher and a group of attentive students; even in these conditions, a geography lesson is possible. But not all Sahara children are lucky enough to go to school.

Education is a major problem in desert areas. In villages where families live all year round, the school is an important institution. Classes are held every day, often under difficult conditions. Though there are neither desks nor pencils, still less any computers, the children are not discouraged.

But some young Saharans never go to school. Most of them are nomads who by definition always wander the desert. Of course, they learn from their parents all kinds of skills necessary for survival: how to find their way though the vast desert, how to care for their animals, and how to find and save water. But increasing numbers of nomads are giving up their way of life to settle in one place and so there are fewer and fewer young people in the Sahara who cannot read or write.

Even today, children of Saharan nomads find it difficult to attend school.

The Formation of the Sahara

These towers of rock reddened by the setting sun in Tassili-oua-n-Ahaggar are strangely informative. They offer us a history of the Sahara and its geology, for their tortured forms have been sculpted by the passage of millions of years.

Strange to think that 420 million years ago, the Sahara lay at the South Pole! Since then, continental drift has very gradually moved the continents apart. Africa reached its current location around 200 million years ago.

During the Mesozoic era (200 to 70 million years ago), the Sahara was completely covered by the sea. The creatures that inhabited the sea died and sank to the ocean floor, their bones and shells slowly forming thick layers. Over millions of years they were compressed into the kind of rock called "sedimentary". Then the ocean withdrew, leaving these rocks exposed to the influence of wind and water, which shaped and dissolved them. This process is called erosion, and sedimentary rocks—such as sandstone and limestone—are particularly vulnerable to it.

The Tassili-oua-n-Ahaggar is a series of flat plains (*plateaux*) of sandstone that have been eroded since the Tertiary era (70 to 15 million years ago). Mountain streams and rivers have dug deep beds through them. Then came drought and with it wind whipping sand against the rock. The softer stone has dissolved and collapsed, leaving harder formations still standing. The result is these towers of solid rock.

Erosion has sculpted spectacular landscapes in the desert.

Djenné Mosque

No concrete here. This mosque, which lies on a bend of the river Niger, is made of mud-bricks dried in the sun and regularly re-coated. The current building dates from 1907.

The conversion to Islam of Africa in general and the Sahara in particular began in the ninth century. The Arabs who overran northern Africa shared their religious beliefs along the trade routes through the desert. Traders and travellers with their camels tended to travel in large groups called "caravans". Muslims following the caravan routes established new kingdoms and religious centres. One of these was Djenné, where the first Great Mosque was built in the thirteenth century. Here Islamic scholars meditated on the teachings of the prophet Muhammad, which are recorded in the Koran.

The architecture of this mosque is remarkable. It rests on ninety pillars, which are invisible behind the thick, mud-brick walls. These walls are studded with curious-looking beams of wood, which act as a framework for the mud-bricks. The bricks are coated with *banco*: clay, cow-dung, straw and mud are mixed together to make a paste that is as supple as modelling clay and which dries hard in the sun. The mosque has to be re-coated every year because torrential rainstorms, rare as they are, do serious damage to the walls.

Declared a UNESCO World Heritage Site in 1988, this mosque continues to receive funds for its maintenance.

Many Saharans are Muslims and pray five times a day.

Prehistorical Art

The rock paintings and inscriptions of Tassili-n-Ajjer tell the story of the people who lived in the Sahara tens of thousands of years ago. The earliest known habitants lived by hunting but also began to domesticate animals, that is, to breed them for their own use.

During the Quaternary era (two million to 10,000 years ago), the climate of the Sahara was not as dry as it is now. Elephants, hippopotamuses and other wild beasts lived on what was then savannah (tropical grassland). The prehistoric inhabitants hunted these animals with bows and spears. They also fished, gathered fruit and berries, and kept herds of cattle.

We know about them thanks to the paintings their artists made on rock faces. Their equipment was rough and ready. To make brown, black or white paint, they ground up the minerals they could find—iron, limestone and schist—and mixed them with water. They sometimes put their hand on the rock and blew paint around it to create an outline. Others used flint tools to cut beautiful drawings of giraffes in the stone.

Then the climate changed. The Sahara became a desert and this prehistoric civilisation disappeared. The French explorer Henri Lhote re-discovered the forgotten masterpieces of the Tassili-n-Ajjer in 1950.

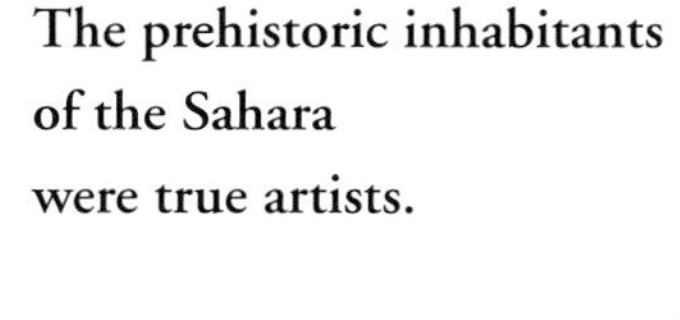

The prehistoric inhabitants of the Sahara were true artists.

The Miracle of Rain on the Plains of Temet

The storm has passed, leaving the soil awash. In a few hours, green shoots cover the plain. Flocks can eat their full. The short rainy season, which affects only a small part of the Sahara, is a period of abundance.

During the rainy season (July to August), a few showers are enough to restore the pastures of the Ténéré region. Once a year, the miracle is accomplished and grass grows. Hidden in the ground, thousands of seeds are waiting for this moment. Among them are many brightly coloured flowers that blossom and wither in just a few days. As many as 2,800 species have been recorded.

Pasture land after rain is called *acheb*. For Saharans, it is a heavenly gift. The Niger herdsmen take their herds to grazing lands in the north during the rainy season. But the season of abundance is short. Within six or eight weeks, the grass will begin to wither and the ponds dry up. The desert again reigns supreme. But all the animals—birds, camels and gazelles—have made the most of it.

In some years, the rainy season never comes. During the last few decades, Niger and Mali have suffered terrible droughts. The result is famine for humans and animals alike.

Flowers await the rain before blossoming in the sand.

Wealth on the Hoof

How proud they look, these *zebu Bororodji* with their curved horns shaped like a Greek lyre! The second part of their name comes from the people who herd them, the Peul Bororo, who have no other wealth than these cattle.

The Peul Bororo own goats and camels but take a particular pride in their cattle. This is their tradition. The Peul Bororo number some 40,000 and have always devoted their lives to cattle. Their wealth is defined by the size of the herds with which they wander over the desert in search of fresh grass. From their cattle comes milk for their sustenance and clothes for their backs. Only the Bororo wear leather trousers in the desert!

The women look after the herds. They milk them morning and night, storing the milk in a *calabash*, a kind of gourd—a large fruit hollowed out and its shell used like a large bowl. The children help them in this work. At six, they are considered old enough to become herders.

Among the Peul Bororo, the important decisions are made by men. They choose the pastures and the best route to them. During a drought, when grass is rare and the cattle are thin, the slightest error can be catastrophic. Their wealth can be reduced to bones whitening in the sun.

Milking cows is a daily activity for the Peul Bororo.

The Land of the Fearless Toubou

Water, water everywhere and not a drop to drink. The metal-blue waters of the lake at Ounianga Kébir are full of salt and bring no prosperity to the 800,000 Toubou who live in northern Chad.

Over a million years ago, these waters were an inland sea. Evaporating in the heat, it became the lake at Ounianga Kébir, whose salty waters are useless for agriculture. The Toubou nomads, who come from the local highlands of Tibesti and Ennedi, wander across this desolate region, which has long been part of their territory.

Scientists consider the Toubou one of the oldest peoples in Africa. Little is known about their history and origins, but some think that they date back to the Stone Age and the arrival of *homo sapiens* (the first modern humans), some 70,000 years ago. We do know that the Toubou have always fearlessly resisted invaders such as the Tuaregs, their neighbours and enemies, and also the Europeans they encountered during the colonial invasions of Africa in the nineteenth century. Hence their reputation as ferocious warriors.

The traditional costume for men is a turban and white clothes: a loose-fitting shirt called a *boubou* and tight trousers. The women wrap themselves elegantly in a multi-coloured veil as much as four metres long. The Toubou are known for their modest needs. Sustained by a mere handful of dates, they cover enormous distances. Their main resource is their cattle, an essential part of the nomad way of life.

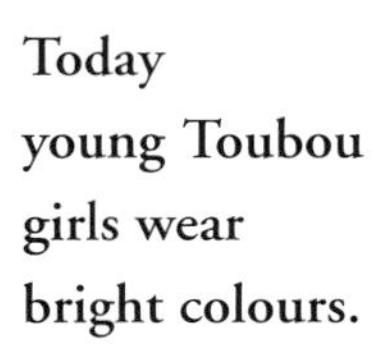

Today young Toubou girls wear bright colours.

The "Blue Mountains" of Izouzadene

A scene from a science-fiction film? The blue rocks seem to be cunningly arranged to mimic the surface of another planet. But this mysterious scene is completely natural.

Throughout the Sahara, nature wildly exceeds the imagination. But at the foot of the Tagmert massif in the Aïr, the stage set is particularly spectacular. It's not every day that you come across blue boulders! This is a natural phenomenon caused by the chemical composition of the stones scattered over this "mineral garden".

The colour is produced by the marble in the boulders. Marble is a sedimentary rock that has been transformed by extreme pressure or heat, such as during a volcanic eruption. That is what happened here. The great heat produced a chemical reaction resulting in the blue veins in these rocks. Daylight causes shimmering reflections on the surface of these shiny rocks.

The Sahara abounds in natural wonders of this kind.

Volcanoes put on fearsome firework displays!

CHAD

A Relic of War

A strange place to leave a tank! This one belonged to the Libyan army and is rusting away in northern Chad. The desert has seen many battles.

The pattern of war is well established. A country wants to conquer its neighbour and therefore seeks a reason for declaring war on it. In the 1980s, Libya thought Chad a very desirable prey, and Libyan troops launched an invasion by crossing the border in the Tibesti region. The conflict dragged on for more than a decade, finally ending in 1994. When the invasion failed, the retreating Libyan army abandoned useless military equipment where it stood.

What was the point of trying to capture an area of empty desert? The answer lies hidden beneath the sand. The Sahara conceals fabulous treasures. There are underground oil and gas reserves in Algeria and Libya, diamond fields in Mauritania, and gold and mineral deposits in several regions. Resources of this kind are very tempting for foreign powers.

The Saharans have been known to revolt against the leadership of their countries. Oppressed and neglected by their national governments, in 1990 the Tuaregs of Niger and Mali took up arms to enforce their rights.

Note the proud demeanour of these Tuareg warriors, bolt upright on their dromedaries.

LIBYA

An Oasis on Lake Oum-el-Ma

A green line stands out on the horizon. It's formed by palm trees and reeds growing next to water. Here they keep at bay the dunes of the Erg of Oubaru in the Fezzan region of Libya. Every oasis is a haven, a safe harbour in the desert.

An oasis suddenly appears in the distance. The nomads stride out towards it. After exhausting hours spent trekking through the dunes, they know that a few hours rest awaits them.

The inhabitants of oases are attracted by the life-giving magic of water. They construct their houses in the shade of oleanders and date palms to form villages and sometimes even large market-towns, like Faya-Largeau (30,000 inhabitants) in Chad. Their gardens are planted with orange trees. The water circulates in irrigation channels, making it possible to cultivate tomatoes, courgettes and other "thirsty" vegetables.

Sometimes, perceiving an oasis in the distance, weary travellers walk on and on without every getting any closer to it. This is a mirage, a phenomenon frequently encountered in the Sahara. The scientific explanation is this: different temperatures of air refract, or bend, light differently. This can create optical illusions, especially when an upside down image of the sky appears like a sheet of glittering water on the horizon. Thirsty travellers hoping to quench their thirst in the sky are doomed to disappointment!

Oases are havens in the desert. Their inhabitants live a sedentary life.

The Inexorable Advance of the Desert

Why would a captain anchor his ship amid the dunes? When the shoreline keeps moving. On the coast of Mauritania, the dunes invade the Atlantic Ocean.

A titanic duel is being fought along the Mauritanian coast. On the one hand, the Atlantic hurls its waves against the shore: on the other, the desert keeps pushing its dunes out into the sea. And for once the land is forcing the sea back. This explains the sight of an old cargo ship rusting away several hundred metres inland.

This extraordinary phenomenon is caused by the trade winds. They blow steadily from the east, from the land out to sea, picking up the sand as they go and driving it on before them. The dunes advance, sometimes quite fast—they may travel as much as ten or fifteen metres a year.

The Sahara as a whole remains where it is. It is only the evocatively named "fields of dunes" that are moved by the prevailing winds, and generally only over very small distances.

The inhabitants of desert cities do not attempt to clear doors and windows buried by the sand.

Master Fishermen

What a magnificent cast! The Bozo fishermen of the Niger excel in the art of wielding the cast-net, their skill has been passed down from generation to generation.

For more than ten centuries the Bozo fishermen have cast their nets where the Bani River flows into the Niger. They number perhaps no more than 10,000, but think of themselves as the undisputed masters of the river. In the past, they lived by hunting the hippopotamuses that once abounded in the Niger. The near extinction of the Niger hippopotamus has forced the Bozo people to change direction and become fishermen. But so great is their skill that one legend says that they can "live underwater and command the fish". They are also known as the "master fishermen".

The Bozo people are Muslims. They live close to the water's edge, though the water-level rises and falls with the rains. They make their own fishing gear, weaving pots like lobster pots out of woven branches to catch fish in, and construct their dug-out canoes from tree-trunks. They generally paddle their canoes, but sometimes use a long pole to make headway against the current. Standing in the prow of his dug-out, the fisherman strikes a noble pose as he casts his net. The Bozo tribe catches some 45,000 tonnes of fish a year. The Niger holds around 140 species, including catfish and the tasty "Captain fish" or Threadfin, which can grow to one hundred kilos in weight. The fish are dried in the sun then sold on the local market at Mopti or transported further afield by lorry.

The Bozo people of the Niger are fishermen.

ALGERIA

The Pole Star Leads the Dance

The white dot at the centre of this celestial dance is the Pole Star, which tells the traveller which way is north. As revealed by this time-lapse photograph, the other stars seem to dance around it.

Sleeping in the open air in the Tassili-n-Ajjer plateau is an unforgettable experience. Thousands of stars glitter intensely in the entirely cloud-free sky. Some of these are grouped in constellations. Astronomers observing the Milky Way gave them evocative names such as the Great Bear, the Dog, and the Southern Cross.

The Saharans too know how to interpret the stars. The Tuareg find their way through the desert with the help of the constellation Orion—they call it *Amanar*, or "guide", in their own language, which is known as Tamahaq.

For the traveller, twilight is the time to set up camp. Then everyone lies down under the stars. After a long day's trekking, the nomads make a fire, cook *tagella* (flat-bread made of wheat) and serve very sweet mint tea. Then they prepare for rest.

A night in the open allows visitors to observe the stars of the southern hemisphere.

Ruins of an Ancient Civilisation

These pyramids, temples and tombs were built in ancient times. The city has been abandoned, but these ruins are one of the great archaeological treasures of Sudan.

The kingdom of Kush existed ten centuries before the current era. Its sovereigns were great builders, who founded two cities in the valley of the upper Nile in Sudan: Napata and Meroe. The wealth of these kings was envied by their northern neighbours in Egypt, who invaded Kush around 2,700 BC.

The victorious Egyptians imposed their own customs and observances in Kush, constructing temples to honour their own divinities. The temple at Soleb is dedicated to Amun, the Sun god. The Egyptians also built pyramids at Meroe and vast cemeteries—like the frescoed tombs of Napata—for their rulers, who were known as pharaohs.

Much later, in the tenth century AD, the region became Islamic. Then it was the turn of the marabouts, the Muslim holy men, to construct funerary monuments; here we see an Islamic mausoleum at Dongola.

The ancient peoples of the Nile were pyramid-builders.

Awaiting the Fertile Waters

This peasant is preparing his field on the banks of the Nile. He digs the earth and raises little dividing walls so that when the river overflows its banks, the trapped flood-water will fertilise the soil.

The Nile is the only river to cross the Sahara. Flowing from the south to the north for over 6,700 kilometres, it finally flows into the Mediterranean. It loses a great deal of water to evaporation during its 3,000-kilometre journey through the desert, but it maintains a steady flow, fed by its inexhaustible sources in the heart of Africa (Burundi and Ethiopia), and by the huge Lake Victoria (whose 68,100 square kilometres of water are divided between Uganda, Kenya and Tanzania). The abundant rain that falls upstream, at the Equator, produces summer floods in the Nile, and for a few weeks it overflows its banks. Then the rich sediment it carries is deposited on the fields of the flood valley in both Sudan and Egypt. This annual event is eagerly awaited by the peasants, who depend on it for a successful harvest.

The fertility of the Nile is one of the main attractions of its banks, their green fertility contrasting so strongly with the arid desert on either side. In ancient times, the Egyptians founded a brilliant civilisation on these shores. Nowadays, the peoples of the Nile still cultivate the soil but depend on tourism to supplement their incomes.

Every year, the Nile floods fertilise the land of the Egyptian peasants.

The Daily Routine of the Womenfolk

This village, on Lake Debo in the Niger Delta, often echoes to the hollow pounding of the pestle. The women prepare millet every day, for it is eaten at every meal.

South of the Sahara lies a semi-arid region called the Sahel, which stretches across Mali, Niger, Chad and Sudan. The climate is still very hot and dry, but the land is not as arid as that of the Sahara and supports tropical grassland vegetation, which can survive on little water. For the inhabitants of the sub-Sahara, this is a vital difference. It allows them to cultivate the land and grow millet, their staple crop.

Millet is perfectly adapted to this environment. It flourishes in poor soil, tolerates high temperatures, and needs little water. It is therefore widely grown throughout the Sahel. In the villages, the women look after the crop. Every day, they pound the millet with a wooden pestle and mortar, then make dry bread or porridge with the millet flour. The animals survive on millet straw. Children play their part in the daily chores, taking on little tasks, helping their parents and looking after children younger than themselves.

On the fringes of the desert, the staple crop is millet.

Volcano in Black and White

Flames have burst forth from the earth's centre. Craters have set up their little black cones. The scene is set in the Tibesti massif, where a snow-white deposit of natron has been laid down over the soil like a carpet.

The Tibesti region in northern Chad lies on a fault-line in the earth's crust. Down the ages, successive volcanic eruptions have marked the landscape. One of them gave rise to the Trou au Natron, an enormous *caldera* (the cauldron shape made when the cone of a volcano collapses inwards). This "cauldron", which is seven kilometres wide and seven hundred metres deep, is thought to have been formed at least forty million years ago. Some five to seven million years ago, molten lava from the centre of the earth boiled up again in the same place, forming these cones of black lava, little pointed hats that litter the centre of the caldera. The lava is very rich in natural sodium-carbonate, or natron. This is a water-retaining salt said to have been used by the Egyptians to dry out mummies before they were embalmed. As it cooled, it created this snowy whiteness.

These volcanoes are now extinct. But there is still sufficient underground heat in the region to create hot springs in which the Toubou love to bathe. The Tibesti and the Algerian Hoggar are the two principal volcanic landscapes of the Sahara.

Tibesti nomads enjoy the hot springs of their volcanic region.

LIBYA

The Old Caravan City of Ghadamis

Deserted streets, abandoned terraces. This city of merchants drowses in isolation. The Saharan caravan trade that allowed this city to thrive has not survived the coming of the modern age.

In the nineteenth century, the city of Ghadamis was an important station on the caravan routes across the Sahara. Merchants crossing the desert would stop there to rest and trade. The city controlled commerce from one side of the desert to the other, from the markets of North Africa to those of Sudan and sub-Saharan Africa.

Through Ghadamis came valuable products from Europe or Arabia: silk, arms, spices, tea, perfume and incense. Back through Ghadamis came the wealth of Africa: millet and other cereals, ivory from elephant tusks, ostrich feathers, gold and even slaves. The colonisation of the Sahara by the major European powers during the late nineteenth century resulted in the creation of national frontiers; this in turn brought down the caravan economy because nomads now had to pass through border posts and pay customs duties on their merchandise.

In the past, only men were allowed to be traders in Ghadamis: Muslim women were forbidden to leave the house. But the terraced roofs of the city, which form a veritable labyrinth, offered an alternative means of moving from house to house.

Depopulated, Ghadamis now has the air of a living museum and has been declared a UNESCO World Heritage Site.

The caravan city of Ghadamis was once the site of exotic markets.

On the Trail of the Peul Bororo

Everything must go with them! At the start of the rainy season in July, the nomadic Peul Bororo set off toward pasturelands recently revived by the rains. The whole family travels together.

At the first rains, the Peul Bororo head for the InGall region in north Niger, where the new grass will soon begin growing. Like the soil from which it grows, the grass on which the herds graze is naturally salty, its roots drawing out of the soil minerals essential to the health of the cattle. Indeed, the voyage is known as the "salt cure".

The members of this family carry all their belongings. They have very few belongings and all of them are essential. They include mats for lying and sleeping on, kitchen utensils, a mortar and pestle for pounding millet grain into flour, and plastic canisters for carrying water. At the camp, women and children dismount and immediately set to work. A *stuudu* must be built for the night: a sort of branch bivouac carried by the donkey. The women erect and dismantle it at every halt.

The Peul Bororo generally strike camp and move on every other day.

Semi-nomadic Bororos on the move with their tent and livestock.

At the Guelta of Archei

For the thirsty camels and their riders, stopping at the Guelta of Archei in the Ennedi in Chad region is a necessity. But it is also a pleasure. This natural bathing-pool never dries out.

A *guelta* is a waterhole excavated in the rock by erosion. The Guelta of Archei is particularly prized for two reasons: because its high cliffs provide shade even when the sun is high in the sky, and because its springs never run dry. An aquifer (a layer of porous rock filled with water) ensures that the spring is perennial. The underground water table was formed more than a million years ago when rain was abundant in the Sahara. It has bubbled up ever since. Camels take a long, long drink: they can take in as much as a hundred and thirty litres at one time and then go several days without drinking.

One of the surprises of the Guelta of Archei is a reptile found in its marshes: the dwarf crocodile! This is surprising because reptiles such as the crocodile generally prefer to live in humid tropical forests. But the crocodile can be found here for almost the same reason as the springs. Their ancestors lived at Archei in prehistoric times, when the Sahara was relatively wet; here the dwarf crocodiles have remained through the passing millenia and the changing climate.

Dwarf crocodiles have survived in the Guelta of Archei.

The Salt-Cure Festival

The painted men are adolescent Peul Bororo travelling with their parents. At the major festival of the year, the adolescents dance the "Dance of Beauty", hoping to win a prize for elegance.

The Peul Bororo are fastidious about their appearance. Their face-painting is modelled on criteria of beauty traditional within the tribe. The men first cover their faces with a layer of powder to lighten the colour of their skin. Then they underline their eyelids with a black substance called kohl to make the whites of their eyes stand out. Lastly, they paint their lips dark in order to bring out the whiteness of their teeth. Thus made up, they take part in the Gerewol, the "Dance of Beauty"—effectively a beauty contest. This festival takes place every year at InGall in the Niger, during the salt cure, when the Peul Bororo and their cattle converge on the green pastures after the first rains.

These festivities attract lots of people. For a young bachelor, they are a sort of marriage market. Taking part in the Yaake, the "Charm Dance", he grimaces and rolls his eyes. These strange expressions are intended to captivate a young woman and perhaps capture her heart.

Young Bororo men make themselves up before taking part in their traditional dances.

Tuareg Crafts and Garments

A camel saddle, a sword in its scabbard, small leather bags: these objects, made and decorated by hand, are very elegant. The Tuaregs are famous for their craftsmanship.

Tuaregs travelling in the Sahara carry a small leather bag containing their money and good-luck charms (amulets). They also need sandals for walking in the sand, scabbards for the swords that they continue to wear in homage to their warrior past, and saddles for their camels. These everyday objects are made in goat or camel skin by local craftsmen.

The Tuaregs also work wood, carving it with a little axe called a *herminette* to make bowls, ladles, spoons, knife-handles and even pulleys for use at deep wells. Blacksmiths work copper, silver and steel. They fashion double-sided blades for the Tuareg chieftains and heavy jewellery for their wives. Over the course of the centuries, the Tuaregs have thus created a remarkably sophisticated art, unlike any other in the Sahara.

The Tuaregs are fine craftsmen and weave beautiful fabrics. These are Tuareg blankets.

Salt Harvest

These waterholes produce a water whose high salt content can be harvested by evaporation. The salt-pans of Teguidda-n-Tesemt, at the foot of the Aïr massif, are among the last in the Sahara still exploited.

Under the salt-pans of Teguiddan-n-Tesemt is a table of salt water, a remnant of the sea that once covered the Sahara in the Mesozoic era. The workers here are salt-makers harvesting the salt. The production method is simple: the salty water is allowed to evaporate in the heat of the sun, the salt crystals forming a fine film on the walls of the pans. The crystals are then shaped into "loaves" of salt in conical, pointed earthenware moulds that also serve to protect the salt. The merchants who buy it then have it carried by camels across the desert towards the markets of Bilma (Niger) and Timbuktu (Mali).

Salt is essential to the human diet both because of its water-retaining properties and because it contains trace elements indispensable to both animals and humans. Niger salt is not of the highest quality and is used only for cattle.

Salt is still transported by caravan.

A Diversity of Sand

With its waves, currents and ever-changing reflections, this might be the sea. And like the sea, the coloured sands of the Adrar massif are shaped and caressed by the wind, the true architect of the desert.

"Who created the desert?" The wind is said to reply "I did", before returning to its endless work. The legend is an accurate reflection of the important role played by the wind in the making of the desert landscape.

For thousands of years, the wind has worn away anything that stands upright in the Sahara. The rocks attacked in this way are of varying hardness. Sandstone and even granite are gradually eroded by the wind's endless onslaught. The stone crumbles into a powder composed of the crystals of quartz that we call grains of sand.

To the naked eye, all grains of sand look alike. But magnification reveals that each is different. Each retains the colours and some of the characteristic shapes of the rocks from which it was worn. A grain of sand can be light or dense, round, spherical or triangular. Under the microscope, its surface is seen to be rough and grainy rather than polished and shiny. And the colour of each grain is different: white, yellow, ochre, pink, red. This delicate palette is part of the magic of the desert.

In the desert, sand is a product of wind-erosion.

The Rhythm of the Camel's Gait

The caravan sets out. The camels will sway onward over the sand, their slow, regular steps continuing till sunset. These are the only animals that can traverse the desert.

The Saharan camel is known as the dromedary, which is a camel with only one hump on its back.

If ever there were a beast constructed specially for the desert, it's the camel, which is strong, hardy and ideally suited to the desert. Camels are herbivores, feeding on grasses and other plants. They have a special liking for acacia thorns and branches, but they can go up to three weeks without eating or drinking. They take their precautions before setting off, eating enough to fill their humps with fat. This is the "storehouse" on which they draw during the voyage. They make an average speed of four to five kilometres an hour and can cover eight hundred kilometres in a fortnight carrying a load of a hundred and fifty kilos. The sight of the dromedary swaying across oceans of sand has given it the nickname "the ship of the desert".

The great caravans loaded with merchandise—these days mostly salt—comprise up to a hundred camels under the careful watch of some ten or more riders. They are a rare sight today, mostly having been replaced by convoys of lorries, which, though they are much faster, cause pollution.

Camels, the "ships of the desert", are true beasts of burden.

Fantastical Chalk Sculptures

Is it a sunshade? A stone mushroom? A magician? Or a ghost? These unimaginable objects are natural sculptures from the White Desert in Egypt.

Nature is a bold and patient artist. It took centuries for these astonishing sculptures in the White Desert—a desert of chalk—to come into being.

Nature's assistant here is sand. Picked up and carried by the wind, it assails the fragile chalk (a sedimentary rock and therefore easily worn down) with its abrasive power. Each grain of quartz is transformed into a tiny tooth nibbling away at the white surface. Slowly the rock is worn away. But this is not done in a uniform manner: the action of the sand is most intense at ground-level, so that the base of the rock is eroded more quickly, resulting here in this strange mushroom shape with its leaning head. The same phenomenon can produce needles or soaring arches in the form of bridges suspended over the desert. The Aloba Arch in Chad is, at eighty metres, the second tallest arch in the world.

The Aloba Arch, at eighty metres, is one of the world's tallest arches in living rock.

The Hardy Acacia

Few trees are tougher than the acacia. It valiantly roots itself in the earth, then raises its leaves to the light, matching their number to the amount of water available in the ground. It too has adapted to the Sahara.

No desert tree can afford to put forth a great canopy of leaves as those we see in the deciduous trees of temperate regions such as Europe. This acacia from the Sendégué region of Mali shows the precautions it takes against sunlight and animals: its leaves are small and bristle with thorns. They also have a sort of natural varnish, which helps prevent the water stored in the leaves from evaporating. The roots, meanwhile, penetrate ever deeper into the ground—up to thirty metres—in search of the slightest drop of moisture. Every form of Saharan plant-life has taken similar precautions for its own survival.

Thanks to these strategies, the acacia is sometimes found in the most hostile spots. In its isolation, it can even become a landmark. In Niger, one such acacia was famous: the "tree of Ténéré" was the only tree in the entire region. It stood on a trail through the middle of the desert and for many years featured on all the local maps. But one day a lorry driver failed to steer around it and the collision uprooted the old tree. It has been replaced with a metal tree while the trunk of the acacia is now in the museum of Niamey, the capital of Niger.

The famous Ténéré tree was uprooted by a truck and has been replaced by a metal landmark.